MznLnx

Missing Links Exam Preps

Exam Prep for

Management of Retail Buying

Friedlander et al..., 1st Edition

The MznLnx Exam Prep is your link from the texbook and lecture to your exams.

The MznLnx Exam Preps are unauthorized and comprehensive reviews of your textbooks.

All material provided by MznLnx and Rico Publications (c) 2010

Textbook publishers and textbook authors do not particpate in or contribute to these reviews.

MznLnx

Rico
Publications

Exam Prep for Management of Retail Buying
1st Edition
Friedlander et al...

Publisher: Raymond Houge
Assistant Editor: Michael Rouger
Text and Cover Designer: Lisa Buckner
Marketing Manager: Sara Swagger
Project Manager, Editorial Production: Jerry Emerson
Art Director: Vernon Lowerui

Product Manager: Dave Mason
Editorial Assitant: Rachel Guzmanji
Pedagogy: Debra Long
Cover Image: Jim Reed/Getty Images
Text and Cover Printer: City Printing, Inc.
Compositor: Media Mix, Inc.

(c) 2010 Rico Publications
ALL RIGHTS RESERVED. No part of this work covered by the copyright may be reproduced or used in any form or by an means--graphic, electronic, or mechanical, including photocopying, recording, taping, Web distribution, information storage, and retrieval systems, or in any other manner--without the written permission of the publisher.

For more information about our products, contact us at:

Dave.Mason@RicoPublications.com

For permission to use material from this text or

product, submit a request online to:

Dave.Mason@RicoPublications.com

Printed in the United States
ISBN:

Contents

CHAPTER 1
An Overview of Retail Buying — 1

CHAPTER 2
The Roles of Buying Groups — 5

CHAPTER 3
Understanding the Consumer — 8

CHAPTER 4
Merchandise Assortments — 13

CHAPTER 5
Planning and Control — 16

CHAPTER 6
Technology and Internet Commerce in Retailing — 18

CHAPTER 7
Choosing Vendors — 22

CHAPTER 8
International Vendors — 24

CHAPTER 9
Translating Plans into Purchases — 27

CHAPTER 10
Negotiating the Buy — 30

CHAPTER 11
The Buyer's Order and Vendor Relations — 34

CHAPTER 12
Pricing and Selling — 39

ANSWER KEY — 44

TO THE STUDENT

COMPREHENSIVE

The *MznLnx* Exam Prep series is designed to help you pass your exams. Editors at MznLnx review your textbooks and then prepare these practice exams to help you master the textbook material. Unlike study guides, workbooks, and practice tests provided by the texbook publisher and textbook authors, *MznLnx* gives you **all** of the material in each chapter in exam form, not just samples, so you can be sure to nail your exam.

MECHANICAL

The MznLnx Exam Prep series creates exams that will help you learn the subject matter as well as test you on your understanding. Each question is designed to help you master the concept. Just working through the exams, you gain an understanding of the subject--its a simple mechanical process that produces success.

INTEGRATED STUDY GUIDE AND REVIEW

MznLnx is not just a set of exams designed to test you, its also a comprehensive review of the subject content. Each exam question is also a review of the concept, making sure that you will get the answer correct without having to go to other sources of material. You learn as you go! Its the easiest way to pass an exam.

HUMOR

Studying can be tedious and dry. MznLnx's instructional design includes moderate humor within the exam questions on occassion, to break the tedium and revitalize the brain

Chapter 1. An Overview of Retail Buying

1. _____ is a broad label that refers to any individuals or households that use goods and services generated within the economy. The concept of a _____ is used in different contexts, so that the usage and significance of the term may vary.

Typically when business people and economists talk of _____s they are talking about person as _____, an aggregated commodity item with little individuality other than that expressed in the buy/not-buy decision.

   a. 28-hour day
   b. Consumer
   c. 1990 Clean Air Act
   d. 33 Strategies of War

2. _____ consists of the sale of goods or merchandise from a fixed location, such as a department store, boutique or kiosk in small or individual lots for direct consumption by the purchaser. _____ may include subordinated services, such as delivery. Purchasers may be individuals or businesses.
   a. Planogram
   b. 28-hour day
   c. 1990 Clean Air Act
   d. Retailing

3. In economics, _____ is the desire to own something and the ability to pay for it. The term _____ signifies the ability or the willingness to buy a particular commodity at a given point of time.
   a. 33 Strategies of War
   b. 28-hour day
   c. 1990 Clean Air Act
   d. Demand

4. _____ is a form of communication that typically attempts to persuade potential customers to purchase or to consume more of a particular brand of product or service. 'While now central to the contemporary global economy and the reproduction of global production networks, it is only quite recently that _____ has been more than a marginal influence on patterns of sales and production. The formation of modern _____ was intimately bound up with the emergence of new forms of monopoly capitalism around the end of the 19th and beginning of the 20th century as one element in corporate strategies to create, organize and where possible control markets, especially for mass produced consumer goods.
   a. A4e
   b. AAAI
   c. Advertising
   d. A Stake in the Outcome

Chapter 1. An Overview of Retail Buying

5. _____ is one of the managerial functions like planning, organizing, staffing and directing. It is an important function because it helps to check the errors and to take the corrective action so that deviation from standards are minimized and stated goals of the organization are achieved in desired manner. According to modern concepts, _____ is a foreseeing action whereas earlier concept of _____ was used only when errors were detected. _____ in management means setting standards, measuring actual performance and taking corrective action.
   a. Turnover
   b. Schedule of reinforcement
   c. Decision tree pruning
   d. Control

6. _____ is one of the four Ps of the marketing mix. The other three aspects are product, promotion, and place. It is also a key variable in microeconomic price allocation theory.
   a. Price floor
   b. Penetration pricing
   c. Transfer pricing
   d. Pricing

7. In a human resources context, _____ or labor _____ is the rate at which an employer gains and loses employees. Simple ways to describe it are 'how long employees tend to stay' or 'the rate of traffic through the revolving door.' _____ is measured for individual companies and for their industry as a whole. If an employer is said to have a high _____ relative to its competitors, it means that employees of that company have a shorter average tenure than those of other companies in the same industry.
   a. Career portfolios
   b. Ten year occupational employment projection
   c. Continuous
   d. Turnover

8. _____, Gross profit margin or Gross Profit Rate can be defined as the amount of contribution to the business enterprise, after paying for direct-fixed and direct-variable unit costs, required to cover overheads (fixed commitments) and provide a buffer for unknown items. It expresses the relationship between gross profit and sales revenue.

It can be expressed in absolute terms:

Gross Profit = Revenue − Cost of Sales

or as the ratio of gross profit to sales revenue, usually in the form of a percentage:

_____ Percentage = (Revenue-Cost of Sales)/Revenue

Cost of Sales includes variable costs and fixed costs directly linked to the product, such as material and labor.

a. Profit margin
b. Gross margin
c. Profit maximization
d. 1990 Clean Air Act

9. _____ is a measure of a company's earning power from ongoing operations, equal to earnings before the deduction of interest payments and income taxes.

To accountants, economic profit, or EP, is a single-period metric to determine the value created by a company in one period - usually a year. It is the net profit after tax less the equity charge, a risk-weighted cost of capital.

a. AAAI
b. A Stake in the Outcome
c. Operating profit
d. A4e

10. In economics, business, retail, and accounting, a _____ is the value of money that has been used up to produce something, and hence is not available for use anymore. In economics, a _____ is an alternative that is given up as a result of a decision. In business, the _____ may be one of acquisition, in which case the amount of money expended to acquire it is counted as _____.

a. Cost allocation
b. Fixed costs
c. Cost overrun
d. Cost

11. _____ is one of the four elements of marketing mix. An organization or set of organizations (go-betweens) involved in the process of making a product or service available for use or consumption by a consumer or business user.

The other three parts of the marketing mix are product, pricing, and promotion.

a. Job creation programs
b. Missing completely at random
c. Matching theory
d. Distribution

12. _____ is a unique identifier for each distinct product and service that can be purchased. Usage of the _____ system is rooted in data management, enabling the merchant to systematically track their inventory, such as in warehouses and retail outlets, and are often assigned and serialized at the merchant level. Each _____ is attached to an item, variant, product line, bundle, service, fee, or attachment.
   a. Stock keeping unit
   b. 28-hour day
   c. 1990 Clean Air Act
   d. 33 Strategies of War

13. In engineering and manufacturing, _____ and quality engineering are used in developing systems to ensure products or services are designed and produced to meet or exceed customer requirements. Refer to the definition by Merriam-Webster for further information . These systems are often developed in conjunction with other business and engineering disciplines using a cross-functional approach.
   a. Statistical process control
   b. Quality control
   c. Single Minute Exchange of Die
   d. Process capability

14. A _____ is a commercial building for storage of goods. _____s are used by manufacturers, importers, exporters, wholesalers, transport businesses, customs, etc. They are usually large plain buildings in industrial areas of cities and towns.
   a. Warehouse
   b. 33 Strategies of War
   c. 1990 Clean Air Act
   d. 28-hour day

15. _____ is a term defined by the Oxford English Dictionary as an individual's 'course or progress through life '. It is usually considered to pertain to remunerative work (and sometimes also formal education.)

The etymology of the term is somewhat ironic in that it comes from the Latin word carrera, which means race .

   a. Spatial mismatch
   b. Nursing shortage
   c. Career planning
   d. Career

Chapter 2. The Roles of Buying Groups

1. _____ consists of the sale of goods or merchandise from a fixed location, such as a department store, boutique or kiosk in small or individual lots for direct consumption by the purchaser. _____ may include subordinated services, such as delivery. Purchasers may be individuals or businesses.
    a. Planogram
    b. 1990 Clean Air Act
    c. 28-hour day
    d. Retailing

2. _____ is a form of communication that typically attempts to persuade potential customers to purchase or to consume more of a particular brand of product or service. 'While now central to the contemporary global economy and the reproduction of global production networks, it is only quite recently that _____ has been more than a marginal influence on patterns of sales and production. The formation of modern _____ was intimately bound up with the emergence of new forms of monopoly capitalism around the end of the 19th and beginning of the 20th century as one element in corporate strategies to create, organize and where possible control markets, especially for mass produced consumer goods.
    a. A4e
    b. A Stake in the Outcome
    c. Advertising
    d. AAAI

3. _____ is an advertisement in which a particular product specifically mentions a competitor by name for the express purpose of showing why the competitor is inferior to the product naming it.

This should not be confused with parody advertisements, where a fictional product is being advertised for the purpose of poking fun at the particular advertisement, nor should it be confused with the use of a coined brand name for the purpose of comparing the product without actually naming an actual competitor. ('Wikipedia tastes better and is less filling than the Encyclopedia Galactica.')

In the 1980s, during what has been referred to as the cola wars, soft-drink manufacturer Pepsi ran a series of advertisements where people, caught on hidden camera, in a blind taste test, chose Pepsi over rival Coca-Cola.

    a. 33 Strategies of War
    b. 28-hour day
    c. Comparative advertising
    d. 1990 Clean Air Act

4. Wholesaling, jobbing to industrial, commercial, institutional or to other _____ and related subordinated services.

According to the United Nations Statistics Division, 'wholesale' is the resale (sale without transformation) of new and used goods to retailers, to industrial, commercial, institutional or professional users or involves acting as an agent or broker in buying merchandise for such persons or companies. _____ frequently physically assemble, sort and grade goods in large lots, break bulk, repack and redistribute in smaller lots.

a. Wholesalers
b. Supply chain
c. Packaging
d. Supply chain management

5. _____ is one of the managerial functions like planning, organizing, staffing and directing. It is an important function because it helps to check the errors and to take the corrective action so that deviation from standards are minimized and stated goals of the organization are achieved in desired manner. According to modern concepts, _____ is a foreseeing action whereas earlier concept of _____ was used only when errors were detected. _____ in management means setting standards, measuring actual performance and taking corrective action.
   a. Decision tree pruning
   b. Turnover
   c. Schedule of reinforcement
   d. Control

6. _____ is one of the four elements of marketing mix. An organization or set of organizations (go-betweens) involved in the process of making a product or service available for use or consumption by a consumer or business user.

The other three parts of the marketing mix are product, pricing, and promotion.

   a. Distribution
   b. Missing completely at random
   c. Job creation programs
   d. Matching theory

7. _____ is one of the four Ps of the marketing mix. The other three aspects are product, promotion, and place. It is also a key variable in microeconomic price allocation theory.
   a. Penetration pricing
   b. Price floor
   c. Transfer pricing
   d. Pricing

8. A _____ is a list of the general tasks and responsibilities of a position. Typically, it also includes to whom the position reports, specifications such as the qualifications needed by the person in the job, salary range for the position, etc. A _____ is usually developed by conducting a job analysis, which includes examining the tasks and sequences of tasks necessary to perform the job.

a. Recruitment Process Insourcing
b. Recruitment advertising
c. Recruitment
d. Job description

Chapter 3. Understanding the Consumer

1. _____ is a broad label that refers to any individuals or households that use goods and services generated within the economy. The concept of a _____ is used in different contexts, so that the usage and significance of the term may vary.

Typically when business people and economists talk of _____s they are talking about person as _____, an aggregated commodity item with little individuality other than that expressed in the buy/not-buy decision.

   a. 28-hour day
   b. 33 Strategies of War
   c. 1990 Clean Air Act
   d. Consumer

2. In economics, _____ is the desire to own something and the ability to pay for it. The term _____ signifies the ability or the willingness to buy a particular commodity at a given point of time.
   a. Demand
   b. 28-hour day
   c. 33 Strategies of War
   d. 1990 Clean Air Act

3. _____ is an integrated communications-based process through which individuals and communities discover that existing and newly-identified needs and wants may be satisfied by the products and services of others.

_____ is defined by the American _____ Association as the activity, set of institutions, and processes for creating, communicating, delivering, and exchanging offerings that have value for customers, clients, partners, and society at large. The term developed from the original meaning which referred literally to going to market, as in shopping, or going to a market to buy or sell goods or services.

   a. Disruptive technology
   b. Market development
   c. Customer relationship management
   d. Marketing

4. The term '_____' refers to the concept of collecting information and attempting to spot a pattern in the information. In some fields of study, the term '_____' has more formally-defined meanings.

In project management _____ is a mathematical technique that uses historical results to predict future outcome.

Chapter 3. Understanding the Consumer

  a. Trend analysis
  b. Least squares
  c. Regression analysis
  d. Stepwise regression

5. _____ or _____ data refers to selected population characteristics as used in government, marketing or opinion research, or the _____ profiles used in such research. Note the distinction from the term 'demography' Commonly-used _____s include race, age, income, disabilities, mobility (in terms of travel time to work or number of vehicles available), educational attainment, home ownership, employment status, and even location.
  a. Abraham Harold Maslow
  b. Demographic
  c. Adam Smith
  d. Affiliation

6. _____ consists of the sale of goods or merchandise from a fixed location, such as a department store, boutique or kiosk in small or individual lots for direct consumption by the purchaser. _____ may include subordinated services, such as delivery. Purchasers may be individuals or businesses.
  a. 1990 Clean Air Act
  b. Planogram
  c. 28-hour day
  d. Retailing

7. A _____ is a measure of the average price of consumer goods and services purchased by households. A _____ measures a price change for a constant market basket of goods and services from one period to the next within the same area (city, region, or nation.) It is a price index determined by measuring the price of a standard group of goods meant to represent the typical market basket of a typical urban consumer.
  a. 28-hour day
  b. 1990 Clean Air Act
  c. 33 Strategies of War
  d. Consumer Price Index

8. _____ is a contract between two parties, one being the employer and the other being the employee. An employee may be defined as: 'A person in the service of another under any contract of hire, express or implied, oral or written, where the employer has the power or right to control and direct the employee in the material details of how the work is to be performed.' Black's Law Dictionary page 471 (5th ed. 1979.)

a. Exit interview
b. Employment rate
c. Employment counsellor
d. Employment

9. In economics, _____s are key economic variables that economists used to predict a new phase of the business cycle. A _____ is one that changes before the economy does; a lagging indicator is one that changes after the economy has changed. Examples of _____s include stock prices, which often improve or worsen before a similar change in the economy.
   a. Leading Indicator
   b. Deflation
   c. Human capital
   d. Perfect competition

10. _____ is a mathematical science pertaining to the collection, analysis, interpretation or explanation, and presentation of data. It also provides tools for prediction and forecasting based on data. It is applicable to a wide variety of academic disciplines, from the natural and social sciences to the humanities, government and business.
    a. Location parameter
    b. Simple moving average
    c. Failure rate
    d. Statistics

11. _____ is a form of communication that typically attempts to persuade potential customers to purchase or to consume more of a particular brand of product or service. 'While now central to the contemporary global economy and the reproduction of global production networks, it is only quite recently that _____ has been more than a marginal influence on patterns of sales and production. The formation of modern _____ was intimately bound up with the emergence of new forms of monopoly capitalism around the end of the 19th and beginning of the 20th century as one element in corporate strategies to create, organize and where possible control markets, especially for mass produced consumer goods.
    a. A4e
    b. AAAI
    c. A Stake in the Outcome
    d. Advertising

12. Marketing research is a form of business research and is generally divided into two categories: consumer _____ and business-to-business (B2B) _____, which was previously known as industrial marketing research. Consumer marketing research studies the buying habits of individual people while business-to-business marketing research investigates the markets for products sold by one business to another.

Chapter 3. Understanding the Consumer 11

Consumer _____ is a form of applied sociology that concentrates on understanding the behaviours, whims and preferences, of consumers in a market-based economy, and aims to understand the effects and comparative success of marketing campaigns.

   a. Questionnaire construction
   b. Questionnaire
   c. Mystery shoppers
   d. Market Research

13. An _____ is an organization founded and funded by businesses that operate in a specific industry. An industry trade association participates in public relations activities such as advertising, education, political donations, lobbying and publishing, but its main focus is collaboration between companies, or standardization. Associations may offer other services, such as producing conferences, networking or charitable events or offering classes or educational materials.
   a. A Stake in the Outcome
   b. A4e
   c. AAAI
   d. Industry trade group

14. _____ is an advertisement in which a particular product specifically mentions a competitor by name for the express purpose of showing why the competitor is inferior to the product naming it.

This should not be confused with parody advertisements, where a fictional product is being advertised for the purpose of poking fun at the particular advertisement, nor should it be confused with the use of a coined brand name for the purpose of comparing the product without actually naming an actual competitor. ('Wikipedia tastes better and is less filling than the Encyclopedia Galactica.')

In the 1980s, during what has been referred to as the cola wars, soft-drink manufacturer Pepsi ran a series of advertisements where people, caught on hidden camera, in a blind taste test, chose Pepsi over rival Coca-Cola.

   a. Comparative advertising
   b. 28-hour day
   c. 1990 Clean Air Act
   d. 33 Strategies of War

15. In probability theory, a probability distribution is called _____ if its cumulative distribution function is _____. This is equivalent to saying that for random variables X with the distribution in question, Pr[X = a] = 0 for all real numbers a, i.e.: the probability that X attains the value a is zero, for any number a. If the distribution of X is _____ then X is called a _____ random variable.

a. Decision tree pruning
b. Pay Band
c. Continuous
d. Connectionist expert systems

16. A _____ is a form of qualitative research in which a group of people are asked about their attitude towards a product, service, concept, advertisement, idea, or packaging. Questions are asked in an interactive group setting where participants are free to talk with other group members.

The first _____s were created at the Bureau of Applied Social Research by associate director, sociologist Robert K. Merton.

a. Market analysis
b. Marketing research
c. 1990 Clean Air Act
d. Focus group

17. In finance, an _____ is a contract between a buyer and a seller that gives the buyer the right--but not the obligation--to buy or to sell a particular asset (the underlying asset) at a later day at an agreed price. In return for granting the _____, the seller collects a payment (the premium) from the buyer. A call _____ gives the buyer the right to buy the underlying asset; a put _____ gives the buyer of the _____ the right to sell the underlying asset.
a. A4e
b. A Stake in the Outcome
c. Option
d. AAAI

Chapter 4. Merchandise Assortments

1. A _____ is a name or trademark connected with a product or producer. _____s have become increasingly important components of culture and the economy, now being described as 'cultural accessories and personal philosophies'.

    Some people distinguish the psychological aspect of a _____ from the experiential aspect.

    a. Brand
    b. Brand extension
    c. Brand loyalty
    d. Brand awareness

2. _____ refers to several different marketing arrangements:

    _____ is when two companies form an alliance to work together, creating marketing synergy. As described in _____: The Science of Alliance:

    _____ is an arrangement that associates a single product or service with more than one brand name, or otherwise associates a product with someone other than the principal producer. The typical _____ agreement involves two or more companies acting in cooperation to associate any of various logos, color schemes, or brand identifiers to a specific product that is contractually designated for this purpose.

    a. 33 Strategies of War
    b. 1990 Clean Air Act
    c. Co-branding
    d. 28-hour day

3. _____ is one of the managerial functions like planning, organizing, staffing and directing. It is an important function because it helps to check the errors and to take the corrective action so that deviation from standards are minimized and stated goals of the organization are achieved in desired manner. According to modern concepts, _____ is a foreseeing action whereas earlier concept of _____ was used only when errors were detected. _____ in management means setting standards, measuring actual performance and taking corrective action.
    a. Schedule of reinforcement
    b. Decision tree pruning
    c. Turnover
    d. Control

4. A _____ is typically described as a deliberate plan of action to guide decisions and achieve rational outcome(s.) However, the term may also be used to denote what is actually done, even though it is unplanned.

    The term may apply to government, private sector organizations and groups, and individuals.

Chapter 4. Merchandise Assortments

    a. 33 Strategies of War
    b. 1990 Clean Air Act
    c. 28-hour day
    d. Policy

5. There are many important decisions about product and service development and marketing. In the process of product development and marketing we should focus on strategic decisions about product attributes, product branding, product packaging, product labeling and product support services. But product strategy also calls for building a _____.
    a. Product bundling
    b. Context analysis
    c. Marketing strategy
    d. Product line

6. In economics, _____ is the desire to own something and the ability to pay for it. The term _____ signifies the ability or the willingness to buy a particular commodity at a given point of time.
    a. 1990 Clean Air Act
    b. 33 Strategies of War
    c. 28-hour day
    d. Demand

7. _____ refers to metrics and measures of output from production processes, per unit of input. Labor _____, for example, is typically measured as a ratio of output per labor-hour, an input. _____ may be conceived of as a metrics of the technical or engineering efficiency of production.
    a. Remanufacturing
    b. Value engineering
    c. Master production schedule
    d. Productivity

8. _____ is a unique identifier for each distinct product and service that can be purchased. Usage of the _____ system is rooted in data management, enabling the merchant to systematically track their inventory, such as in warehouses and retail outlets, and are often assigned and serialized at the merchant level. Each _____ is attached to an item, variant, product line, bundle, service, fee, or attachment.
    a. 1990 Clean Air Act
    b. 33 Strategies of War
    c. 28-hour day
    d. Stock keeping unit

Chapter 4. Merchandise Assortments

9. _____ Management is the succession of strategies used by management as a product goes through its _____. The conditions in which a product is sold changes over time and must be managed as it moves through its succession of stages.

The _____ goes through many phases, involves many professional disciplines, and requires many skills, tools and processes.

   a. Strategic Alliance
   b. Product life cycle
   c. Job hunting
   d. Golden handshake

Chapter 5. Planning and Control

1. _____ is one of the managerial functions like planning, organizing, staffing and directing. It is an important function because it helps to check the errors and to take the corrective action so that deviation from standards are minimized and stated goals of the organization are achieved in desired manner. According to modern concepts, _____ is a foreseeing action whereas earlier concept of _____ was used only when errors were detected. _____ in management means setting standards, measuring actual performance and taking corrective action.
    a. Turnover
    b. Decision tree pruning
    c. Schedule of reinforcement
    d. Control

2. _____ is a unique identifier for each distinct product and service that can be purchased. Usage of the _____ system is rooted in data management, enabling the merchant to systematically track their inventory, such as in warehouses and retail outlets, and are often assigned and serialized at the merchant level. Each _____ is attached to an item, variant, product line, bundle, service, fee, or attachment.
    a. 33 Strategies of War
    b. 1990 Clean Air Act
    c. 28-hour day
    d. Stock keeping unit

3. In a human resources context, _____ or labor _____ is the rate at which an employer gains and loses employees. Simple ways to describe it are 'how long employees tend to stay' or 'the rate of traffic through the revolving door.' _____ is measured for individual companies and for their industry as a whole. If an employer is said to have a high _____ relative to its competitors, it means that employees of that company have a shorter average tenure than those of other companies in the same industry.
    a. Career portfolios
    b. Continuous
    c. Ten year occupational employment projection
    d. Turnover

4. _____ refers to metrics and measures of output from production processes, per unit of input. Labor _____, for example, is typically measured as a ratio of output per labor-hour, an input. _____ may be conceived of as a metrics of the technical or engineering efficiency of production.
    a. Productivity
    b. Master production schedule
    c. Remanufacturing
    d. Value engineering

Chapter 5. Planning and Control

5. In probability theory, a probability distribution is called _____ if its cumulative distribution function is _____. This is equivalent to saying that for random variables X with the distribution in question, Pr[X = a] = 0 for all real numbers a, i.e.: the probability that X attains the value a is zero, for any number a. If the distribution of X is _____ then X is called a _____ random variable.

   a. Decision tree pruning
   b. Connectionist expert systems
   c. Continuous
   d. Pay Band

6. _____, Gross profit margin or Gross Profit Rate can be defined as the amount of contribution to the business enterprise, after paying for direct-fixed and direct-variable unit costs, required to cover overheads (fixed commitments) and provide a buffer for unknown items. It expresses the relationship between gross profit and sales revenue.

It can be expressed in absolute terms:

Gross Profit = Revenue − Cost of Sales

or as the ratio of gross profit to sales revenue, usually in the form of a percentage:

_____ Percentage = (Revenue-Cost of Sales)/Revenue

Cost of Sales includes variable costs and fixed costs directly linked to the product, such as material and labor.

   a. 1990 Clean Air Act
   b. Profit maximization
   c. Profit margin
   d. Gross margin

Chapter 6. Technology and Internet Commerce in Retailing

1. _____, commonly known as e-commerce, consists of the buying and selling of products or services over electronic systems such as the Internet and other computer networks. The amount of trade conducted electronically has grown extraordinarily with widespread Internet usage. The use of commerce is conducted in this way, spurring and drawing on innovations in electronic funds transfer, supply chain management, Internet marketing, online transaction processing, electronic data interchange (EDI), inventory management systems, and automated data collection systems.
   a. A Stake in the Outcome
   b. Online shopping
   c. A4e
   d. Electronic Commerce

2. _____ is an advertisement in which a particular product specifically mentions a competitor by name for the express purpose of showing why the competitor is inferior to the product naming it.

   This should not be confused with parody advertisements, where a fictional product is being advertised for the purpose of poking fun at the particular advertisement, nor should it be confused with the use of a coined brand name for the purpose of comparing the product without actually naming an actual competitor. ('Wikipedia tastes better and is less filling than the Encyclopedia Galactica.')

   In the 1980s, during what has been referred to as the cola wars, soft-drink manufacturer Pepsi ran a series of advertisements where people, caught on hidden camera, in a blind taste test, chose Pepsi over rival Coca-Cola.

   a. 28-hour day
   b. 1990 Clean Air Act
   c. 33 Strategies of War
   d. Comparative advertising

3. A barcode (also bar code) is an optical machine-readable representation of data. Originally, _____ represented data in the widths (lines) and the spacings of parallel lines, and may be referred to as linear or 1D (1 dimensional) barcodes or symbologies. They also come in patterns of squares, dots, hexagons and other geometric patterns within images termed 2D (2 dimensional) matrix codes or symbologies.
   a. 1990 Clean Air Act
   b. Bar codes
   c. 33 Strategies of War
   d. 28-hour day

4. A _____ is an executive position whose holder is focused on scientific and technical issues within an organization. Essentially, a _____ is responsible for the transformation of capital - be it monetary, intellectual, or political - into technology in furtherance of the company's objectives.

   The title is most typically found in organizations which significantly develop or exploit information technology.

Chapter 6. Technology and Internet Commerce in Retailing

a. General Manager
b. Chief knowledge officer
c. Managing director
d. Chief technology officer

5. The _____ is a barcode symbology (i.e., a specific type of barcode), that is widely used in the United States and Canada for tracking trade items in stores. In the _____-A barcode, each digit is represented by a seven-bit sequence, encoded by a series of alternating bars and spaces. Guard bars, shown in green, separate the two groups of six digits.

The _____ encodes 12 decimal digits as SLLLLLLMRRRRRRE, where S (start) and E (end) are the bit pattern 101, M (middle) is the bit pattern 01010 (called guard bars), and each L (left) and R (right) are digits, each one represented by a seven-bit code.

a. A4e
b. AAAI
c. A Stake in the Outcome
d. Universal Product Code

6. _____ is a unique identifier for each distinct product and service that can be purchased. Usage of the _____ system is rooted in data management, enabling the merchant to systematically track their inventory, such as in warehouses and retail outlets, and are often assigned and serialized at the merchant level. Each _____ is attached to an item, variant, product line, bundle, service, fee, or attachment.

a. 1990 Clean Air Act
b. Stock keeping unit
c. 33 Strategies of War
d. 28-hour day

7. _____ refers to the structured transmission of data between organizations by electronic means. It is used to transfer electronic documents from one computer system to another (ie) from one trading partner to another trading partner. It is more than mere E-mail; for instance, organizations might replace bills of lading and even checks with appropriate _____ messages.

a. Electronic Data Interchange
b. A Stake in the Outcome
c. AAAI
d. A4e

8. _____ is an inventory strategy that strives to improve the return on investment of a business by reducing in-process inventory and its associated carrying costs. To meet _____ objectives, the process relies on signals between different points in the process. This means the process is often driven by a series of signals, or Kanban , which tell production when to make the next part. Kanban are usually 'tickets' but can be simple visual signals, such as the presence or absence of a part on a shelf. Implemented correctly, _____ can dramatically improve a manufacturing organization's return on investment, quality, and efficiency.

   a. 1990 Clean Air Act
   b. 28-hour day
   c. 33 Strategies of War
   d. Just-in-time

9. _____ or lean production, which is often known simply as 'Lean', is a production practice that considers the expenditure of resources for any goal other than the creation of value for the end customer to be wasteful, and thus a target for elimination. Working from the perspective of the customer who consumes a product or service, 'value' is defined as any action or process that a customer would be willing to pay for. Basically, lean is centered around creating more value with less work.

   a. Theory of constraints
   b. Production line
   c. Six Sigma
   d. Lean manufacturing

10. _____ is a family of business models in which the buyer of a product provides certain information to a supplier of that product and the supplier takes full responsibility for maintaining an agreed inventory of the material, usually at the buyer's consumption location (usually a store.) A third party logistics provider can also be involved to make sure that the buyer has the required level of inventory by adjusting the demand and supply gaps.

    As a symbiotic relationship, _____ makes it less likely that a business will unintentionally become out of stock of a good and reduces inventory in the supply chain.

    a. Supply Chain Risk Management
    b. Delayed differentiation
    c. Supply-Chain Operations Reference
    d. Vendor Managed Inventory

11. _____ is the difference between the cost of a good or service and its selling price. A _____ is added on to the total cost incurred by the producer of a good or service in order to create a profit. The total cost reflects the total amount of both fixed and variable expenses to produce and distribute a product.

a. Price points
b. Markup
c. Premium pricing
d. Topics

12. _____ is an integrated communications-based process through which individuals and communities discover that existing and newly-identified needs and wants may be satisfied by the products and services of others.

_____ is defined by the American _____ Association as the activity, set of institutions, and processes for creating, communicating, delivering, and exchanging offerings that have value for customers, clients, partners, and society at large. The term developed from the original meaning which referred literally to going to market, as in shopping, or going to a market to buy or sell goods or services.

a. Disruptive technology
b. Customer relationship management
c. Market development
d. Marketing

13. _____ is a broad label that refers to any individuals or households that use goods and services generated within the economy. The concept of a _____ is used in different contexts, so that the usage and significance of the term may vary.

Typically when business people and economists talk of _____s they are talking about person as _____, an aggregated commodity item with little individuality other than that expressed in the buy/not-buy decision.

a. Consumer
b. 1990 Clean Air Act
c. 33 Strategies of War
d. 28-hour day

Chapter 7. Choosing Vendors

1. In marketing, _____ is the process of distinguishing the differences of a product or offering from others, to make it more attractive to a particular target market. This involves differentiating it from competitors' products as well as one's own product offerings.
    a. PEST analysis
    b. Market share
    c. Market development
    d. Product differentiation

2. _____ is one of the four elements of marketing mix. An organization or set of organizations (go-betweens) involved in the process of making a product or service available for use or consumption by a consumer or business user.

The other three parts of the marketing mix are product, pricing, and promotion.

    a. Missing completely at random
    b. Matching theory
    c. Distribution
    d. Job creation programs

3. A _____ is a name or trademark connected with a product or producer. _____s have become increasingly important components of culture and the economy, now being described as 'cultural accessories and personal philosophies'.

Some people distinguish the psychological aspect of a _____ from the experiential aspect.

    a. Brand loyalty
    b. Brand awareness
    c. Brand extension
    d. Brand

4. _____ is one of the four Ps of the marketing mix. The other three aspects are product, promotion, and place. It is also a key variable in microeconomic price allocation theory.
    a. Transfer pricing
    b. Penetration pricing
    c. Pricing
    d. Price floor

Chapter 7. Choosing Vendors

5. _____ is a form of communication that typically attempts to persuade potential customers to purchase or to consume more of a particular brand of product or service. 'While now central to the contemporary global economy and the reproduction of global production networks, it is only quite recently that _____ has been more than a marginal influence on patterns of sales and production. The formation of modern _____ was intimately bound up with the emergence of new forms of monopoly capitalism around the end of the 19th and beginning of the 20th century as one element in corporate strategies to create, organize and where possible control markets, especially for mass produced consumer goods.
   a. A4e
   b. Advertising
   c. A Stake in the Outcome
   d. AAAI

6. Wholesaling, jobbing to industrial, commercial, institutional or to other _____ and related subordinated services.

According to the United Nations Statistics Division, 'wholesale' is the resale (sale without transformation) of new and used goods to retailers, to industrial, commercial, institutional or professional users or involves acting as an agent or broker in buying merchandise for such persons or companies. _____ frequently physically assemble, sort and grade goods in large lots, break bulk, repack and redistribute in smaller lots.

   a. Supply chain management
   b. Packaging
   c. Supply chain
   d. Wholesalers

Chapter 8. International Vendors

1. _____ is a type of trade policy that allows traders to act and transact without interference from government. Thus, the policy permits trading partners mutual gains from trade, with goods and services produced according to the theory of comparative advantage.

Under a _____ policy, prices are a reflection of true supply and demand, and are the sole determinant of resource allocation.

   a. 33 Strategies of War
   b. 1990 Clean Air Act
   c. 28-hour day
   d. Free trade

2. A _____ or transnational corporation is a corporation or enterprise that manages production or delivers services in more than one country. It can also be referred to as an international corporation.

The first modern _____ is generally thought to be the Dutch East India Company, established in 1602.

   a. Financial Accounting Standards Board
   b. Multinational corporation
   c. Small and medium enterprises
   d. Command center

3. _____ is a designated group of countries that have agreed to eliminate tariffs, quotas and preferences on most (if not all) goods and services traded between them. It can be considered the second stage of economic integration. Countries choose this kind of economic integration form if their economical structures are complementary.
   a. 28-hour day
   b. 33 Strategies of War
   c. 1990 Clean Air Act
   d. Free trade area

4. The _____ is a trilateral trade bloc in North America created by the governments of the United States, Canada, and Mexico. The agreement creating the trade bloc came into force on January 1, 1994. It superseded the Canada-United States Free Trade Agreement between the U.S. and Canada.
   a. North American Free Trade Agreement
   b. Trade union
   c. Career portfolios
   d. Business war game

Chapter 8. International Vendors

5. A Purchasing Manager is an employee within a company, business or other organization who is responsible at some level for buying or approving the acquisition of goods and services needed by the company. The position responsibilities may be the same as that of a buyer or _____, or may include wider supervisory or managerial responsibilities. A Purchasing Manager may oversee the acquisition of materials needed for production, general supplies for offices and facilities, equipment, or construction contracts.
    a. Purchasing manager
    b. CEO
    c. Director of communications
    d. Purchasing agent

6. _____ is an advertisement in which a particular product specifically mentions a competitor by name for the express purpose of showing why the competitor is inferior to the product naming it.

This should not be confused with parody advertisements, where a fictional product is being advertised for the purpose of poking fun at the particular advertisement, nor should it be confused with the use of a coined brand name for the purpose of comparing the product without actually naming an actual competitor. ('Wikipedia tastes better and is less filling than the Encyclopedia Galactica.')

In the 1980s, during what has been referred to as the cola wars, soft-drink manufacturer Pepsi ran a series of advertisements where people, caught on hidden camera, in a blind taste test, chose Pepsi over rival Coca-Cola.

    a. 1990 Clean Air Act
    b. 33 Strategies of War
    c. Comparative advertising
    d. 28-hour day

7. _____ is one of the managerial functions like planning, organizing, staffing and directing. It is an important function because it helps to check the errors and to take the corrective action so that deviation from standards are minimized and stated goals of the organization are achieved in desired manner. According to modern concepts, _____ is a foreseeing action whereas earlier concept of _____ was used only when errors were detected. _____ in management means setting standards, measuring actual performance and taking corrective action.
    a. Schedule of reinforcement
    b. Control
    c. Turnover
    d. Decision tree pruning

8. In economics, business, retail, and accounting, a _____ is the value of money that has been used up to produce something, and hence is not available for use anymore. In economics, a _____ is an alternative that is given up as a result of a decision. In business, the _____ may be one of acquisition, in which case the amount of money expended to acquire it is counted as _____.

a. Fixed costs
b. Cost overrun
c. Cost allocation
d. Cost

9. _____ is an initialism which deals with the shipping of goods. Depending on specific usage, it may stand for _____ or Freight On Board, with similar but distinct implications. _____ specifies which party (buyer or seller) pays for which shipment and loading costs, and/or where responsibility for the goods is transferred.
   a. 33 Strategies of War
   b. 1990 Clean Air Act
   c. 28-hour day
   d. Free on board

Chapter 9. Translating Plans into Purchases

1. The _____ is an organization that conducts food safety, public affairs, education, research, and industry relations programs for food retailers and wholesalers. _____'s membership consists of approximately 1,500 companies in 50 countries, ranging from large multi-chain stores to independent supermarkets. In the U.S., _____ members operate some 26,000 retail food stores and 14,000 pharmacies and account for about three quarters of all domestic retail food sales.
    a. Food Marketing Institute
    b. National Whistleblower Center
    c. National Association of Corporate Directors
    d. Limited liability partnership

2. _____ is an integrated communications-based process through which individuals and communities discover that existing and newly-identified needs and wants may be satisfied by the products and services of others.

    _____ is defined by the American _____ Association as the activity, set of institutions, and processes for creating, communicating, delivering, and exchanging offerings that have value for customers, clients, partners, and society at large. The term developed from the original meaning which referred literally to going to market, as in shopping, or going to a market to buy or sell goods or services.

    a. Marketing
    b. Customer relationship management
    c. Disruptive technology
    d. Market development

3. _____ consists of the mental process of thinking involved with the process of judging the merits of multiple options and selecting one of them for action. Some simple examples include deciding whether to get up in the morning or go back to sleep, or selecting a given route for a journey. More complex examples (often decisions that affect what a person thinks or their core beliefs) include choosing a lifestyle, religious affiliation, or political position.
    a. Choice
    b. Groups decision making
    c. Trade study
    d. Championship mobilization

4. The term '_____' refers to the concept of collecting information and attempting to spot a pattern in the information. In some fields of study, the term '_____' has more formally-defined meanings.

    In project management _____ is a mathematical technique that uses historical results to predict future outcome.

a. Regression analysis
b. Stepwise regression
c. Least squares
d. Trend analysis

5. In economics, _____ is a measure of the relative satisfaction from consumption of various goods and services. Given this measure, one may speak meaningfully of increasing or decreasing _____, and thereby explain economic behavior in terms of attempts to increase one's _____. For illustrative purposes, changes in _____ are sometimes expressed in units called utils.

a. Utility
b. A Stake in the Outcome
c. Ordinal utility
d. Indirect utility function

6. _____ is the science, art and technology of enclosing or protecting products for distribution, storage, sale, and use. _____ also refers to the process of design, evaluation, and production of packages. _____ can be described as a coordinated system of preparing goods for transport, warehousing, logistics, sale, and end use.

a. Supply chain
b. Supply chain management
c. Wholesalers
d. Packaging

7. An _____ is the negative aspects of human activity on the biophysical environment. Environmentalism, a social and environmental movement that started in the 1960s, focuses on addressing _____s through advocacy, education and activism.

Major current _____s are climate change, pollution and resource depletion.

a. AAAI
b. A4e
c. A Stake in the Outcome
d. Environmental issue

8. The _____ also known as nature conservation is a political, social and, to some extent, scientific movement that seeks to protect natural resources including plant and animal species as well as their habitat for the future.

Chapter 9. Translating Plans into Purchases

The early _____ not included fisheries and wildlife management, water, soil conservation and sustainable forestry. The contemporary _____ has broadened from the early movement's emphasis on use of sustainable yield of natural resources and preservation of wilderness areas to include preservation of biodiversity.

a. 1990 Clean Air Act
b. 33 Strategies of War
c. Conservation movement
d. 28-hour day

9. Marketing research is a form of business research and is generally divided into two categories: consumer _____ and business-to-business (B2B) _____, which was previously known as industrial marketing research. Consumer marketing research studies the buying habits of individual people while business-to-business marketing research investigates the markets for products sold by one business to another.

Consumer _____ is a form of applied sociology that concentrates on understanding the behaviours, whims and preferences, of consumers in a market-based economy, and aims to understand the effects and comparative success of marketing campaigns.

a. Questionnaire construction
b. Questionnaire
c. Market research
d. Mystery shoppers

10. According to the American Marketing Association, _____ is the marketing of products that are presumed to be environmentally safe. Thus _____ incorporates a broad range of activities, including product modification, changes to the production process, packaging changes, as well as modifying advertising. Yet defining _____ is not a simple task where several meanings intersect and contradict each other; an example of this will be the existence of varying social, environmental and retail definitions attached to this term.

a. SWOT analysis
b. Market share
c. Green marketing
d. Value chain

Chapter 10. Negotiating the Buy

1. _____ consists of the sale of goods or merchandise from a fixed location, such as a department store, boutique or kiosk in small or individual lots for direct consumption by the purchaser. _____ may include subordinated services, such as delivery. Purchasers may be individuals or businesses.
   a. 28-hour day
   b. Retailing
   c. Planogram
   d. 1990 Clean Air Act

2. The _____ of 1936 (or Anti-Price Discrimination Act, 15 U.S.C. § 13) is a United States federal law that prohibits what were considered, at the time of passage, to be anticompetitive practices by producers, specifically price discrimination. It grew out of practices in which chain stores were allowed to purchase goods at lower prices than other retailers.
   a. Labor Management Reporting and Disclosure Act
   b. Privity
   c. Bona fide occupational qualification
   d. Robinson-Patman Act

3. _____ refers to the difference between the cost of materials purchased by a company plus the cost of the labor to assemble a product and the price at which the company sells the product. An example is the price of gasoline at the pump over the price of the oil in it. In national accounts used in macroeconomics, it refers to the contribution of the factors of production, i.e., land, labor, and capital goods, to raising the value of a product and corresponds to the incomes received by the owners of these factors.
   a. Deregulation
   b. Value added
   c. Rehn-Meidner Model
   d. Minimum wage

4. A _____ is popular as a telecommunications industry term for non-core services or, in short, all services beyond standard voice calls and fax transmissions but, it can be used in ANY service industry (eg. Web 2.0) for the services providers provide for no cost to promote their main service business. In telecommunication industry on a conceptual level, _____s add value to the standard service offering, spurring the subscriber to use their phone more and allowing the operator to drive up their ARPU.
   a. 28-hour day
   b. 1990 Clean Air Act
   c. 33 Strategies of War
   d. Value-added service

5. _____ is an advertisement in which a particular product specifically mentions a competitor by name for the express purpose of showing why the competitor is inferior to the product naming it.

Chapter 10. Negotiating the Buy

This should not be confused with parody advertisements, where a fictional product is being advertised for the purpose of poking fun at the particular advertisement, nor should it be confused with the use of a coined brand name for the purpose of comparing the product without actually naming an actual competitor. ('Wikipedia tastes better and is less filling than the Encyclopedia Galactica.')

In the 1980s, during what has been referred to as the cola wars, soft-drink manufacturer Pepsi ran a series of advertisements where people, caught on hidden camera, in a blind taste test, chose Pepsi over rival Coca-Cola.

- a. 1990 Clean Air Act
- b. Comparative advertising
- c. 33 Strategies of War
- d. 28-hour day

6. Wholesaling, jobbing to industrial, commercial, institutional or to other _____ and related subordinated services.

According to the United Nations Statistics Division, 'wholesale' is the resale (sale without transformation) of new and used goods to retailers, to industrial, commercial, institutional or professional users or involves acting as an agent or broker in buying merchandise for such persons or companies. _____ frequently physically assemble, sort and grade goods in large lots, break bulk, repack and redistribute in smaller lots.

- a. Supply chain management
- b. Supply chain
- c. Packaging
- d. Wholesalers

7. The _____ is an independent agency of the United States government, established in 1914 by the _____ Act. Its principal mission is the promotion of 'consumer protection' and the elimination and prevention of what regulators perceive to be harmfully 'anti-competitive' business practices, such as coercive monopoly.

The _____ Act was one of President Wilson's major acts against trusts.

- a. 28-hour day
- b. 33 Strategies of War
- c. 1990 Clean Air Act
- d. Federal Trade Commission

Chapter 10. Negotiating the Buy

8. _____ is an initialism which deals with the shipping of goods. Depending on specific usage, it may stand for _____ or Freight On Board, with similar but distinct implications. _____ specifies which party (buyer or seller) pays for which shipment and loading costs, and/or where responsibility for the goods is transferred.
   a. 1990 Clean Air Act
   b. 33 Strategies of War
   c. Free on board
   d. 28-hour day

9. In economics, business, retail, and accounting, a _____ is the value of money that has been used up to produce something, and hence is not available for use anymore. In economics, a _____ is an alternative that is given up as a result of a decision. In business, the _____ may be one of acquisition, in which case the amount of money expended to acquire it is counted as _____.
   a. Cost
   b. Cost overrun
   c. Fixed costs
   d. Cost allocation

10. _____ is a form of communication that typically attempts to persuade potential customers to purchase or to consume more of a particular brand of product or service. 'While now central to the contemporary global economy and the reproduction of global production networks, it is only quite recently that _____ has been more than a marginal influence on patterns of sales and production. The formation of modern _____ was intimately bound up with the emergence of new forms of monopoly capitalism around the end of the 19th and beginning of the 20th century as one element in corporate strategies to create, organize and where possible control markets, especially for mass produced consumer goods.
   a. AAAI
   b. A Stake in the Outcome
   c. A4e
   d. Advertising

11. _____ is the science, art and technology of enclosing or protecting products for distribution, storage, sale, and use. _____ also refers to the process of design, evaluation, and production of packages. _____ can be described as a coordinated system of preparing goods for transport, warehousing, logistics, sale, and end use.
   a. Packaging
   b. Supply chain management
   c. Supply chain
   d. Wholesalers

12. _____ is a lightweight markup language, originally created by John Gruber and Aaron Swartz to help maximum readability and 'publishability' of both its input and output forms. The language takes many cues from existing conventions for marking up plain text in email. _____ converts its marked-up text input to valid, well-formed XHTML and replaces left-pointing angle brackets ('<') and ampersands with their corresponding character entity references.

   a. 33 Strategies of War
   b. 28-hour day
   c. 1990 Clean Air Act
   d. Markdown

13. A _____ strategy targets non-buying customers in currently targeted segments. It also targets new customers in new segments. (Winer)

A marketing manager has to think about the following questions before implementing a _____ strategy: Is it profitable? Will it require the introduction of new or modified products? Is the customer and channel well enough researched and understood?

The marketing manager uses these four groups to give more focus to the market segment decision: existing customers, competitor customers, non-buying in current segments, new segments.

   a. Market Development
   b. Customer relationship management
   c. Product line
   d. Context analysis

14. Procter is a surname, and may also refer to:

   - Bryan Waller Procter (pseud. Barry Cornwall), English poet
   - Goodwin Procter, American law firm
   - _____, consumer products multinational

   a. Strict liability
   b. Downstream
   c. Procter ' Gamble
   d. Master and Servant Acts

Chapter 11. The Buyer's Order and Vendor Relations

1. _____ is a lightweight markup language, originally created by John Gruber and Aaron Swartz to help maximum readability and 'publishability' of both its input and output forms. The language takes many cues from existing conventions for marking up plain text in email. _____ converts its marked-up text input to valid, well-formed XHTML and replaces left-pointing angle brackets ('<') and ampersands with their corresponding character entity references.

   a. 1990 Clean Air Act
   b. 33 Strategies of War
   c. Markdown
   d. 28-hour day

2. _____ is one of the four Ps of the marketing mix. The other three aspects are product, promotion, and place. It is also a key variable in microeconomic price allocation theory.

   a. Penetration pricing
   b. Pricing
   c. Price floor
   d. Transfer pricing

3. _____ is a form of communication that typically attempts to persuade potential customers to purchase or to consume more of a particular brand of product or service. 'While now central to the contemporary global economy and the reproduction of global production networks, it is only quite recently that _____ has been more than a marginal influence on patterns of sales and production. The formation of modern _____ was intimately bound up with the emergence of new forms of monopoly capitalism around the end of the 19th and beginning of the 20th century as one element in corporate strategies to create, organize and where possible control markets, especially for mass produced consumer goods.

   a. AAAI
   b. A Stake in the Outcome
   c. A4e
   d. Advertising

4. In marketing a _____ is a ticket or document that can be exchanged for a financial discount or rebate when purchasing a product. Customarily, _____s are issued by manufacturers of consumer packaged goods or by retailers, to be used in retail stores as a part of sales promotions. They are often widely distributed through mail, magazines, newspapers, the Internet, and mobile devices such as cell phones.

   a. Word of mouth
   b. Sales promotion
   c. 1990 Clean Air Act
   d. Coupon

5. The United States Federal _____ to oversee the safety of food, drugs, and cosmetics. A principal author of this law was Royal S. Copeland, a three-term U.S. Senator from New York. In 1968, the Electronic Product Radiation Control provisions were added to the FD'C.

a. Food, Drug, and Cosmetic Act
b. Partnership
c. Comprehensive Environmental Response, Compensation, and Liability Act
d. Rulemaking

6. _____ is the science, art and technology of enclosing or protecting products for distribution, storage, sale, and use. _____ also refers to the process of design, evaluation, and production of packages. _____ can be described as a coordinated system of preparing goods for transport, warehousing, logistics, sale, and end use.
   a. Supply chain
   b. Wholesalers
   c. Supply chain management
   d. Packaging

7. The _____ is an independent agency of the United States government, established in 1914 by the _____ Act. Its principal mission is the promotion of 'consumer protection' and the elimination and prevention of what regulators perceive to be harmfully 'anti-competitive' business practices, such as coercive monopoly.

The _____ Act was one of President Wilson's major acts against trusts.

   a. 1990 Clean Air Act
   b. 28-hour day
   c. 33 Strategies of War
   d. Federal Trade Commission

8. The _____ of 1914 (15 U.S.C §§ 41-58, as amended) established the Federal Trade Commission (FTC), a bipartisan body of five members appointed by the President of the United States for seven year terms. This Commission was authorized to issue Cease and Desist orders to large corporations to curb unfair trade practices. This Act also gave more flexibility to the US congress for judicial matters.
   a. Sarbanes-Oxley Act of 2002
   b. Federal Trade Commission Act
   c. Comprehensive Environmental Response, Compensation, and Liability Act
   d. Resource Conservation and Recovery Act

9. _____ is a unique identifier for each distinct product and service that can be purchased. Usage of the _____ system is rooted in data management, enabling the merchant to systematically track their inventory, such as in warehouses and retail outlets, and are often assigned and serialized at the merchant level. Each _____ is attached to an item, variant, product line, bundle, service, fee, or attachment.

a. 28-hour day
b. 1990 Clean Air Act
c. Stock keeping unit
d. 33 Strategies of War

10. The _____ of 1936 (or Anti-Price Discrimination Act, 15 U.S.C. Â§ 13) is a United States federal law that prohibits what were considered, at the time of passage, to be anticompetitive practices by producers, specifically price discrimination. It grew out of practices in which chain stores were allowed to purchase goods at lower prices than other retailers.

a. Privity
b. Bona fide occupational qualification
c. Labor Management Reporting and Disclosure Act
d. Robinson-Patman Act

11. _____ is an advertisement in which a particular product specifically mentions a competitor by name for the express purpose of showing why the competitor is inferior to the product naming it.

This should not be confused with parody advertisements, where a fictional product is being advertised for the purpose of poking fun at the particular advertisement, nor should it be confused with the use of a coined brand name for the purpose of comparing the product without actually naming an actual competitor. ('Wikipedia tastes better and is less filling than the Encyclopedia Galactica.')

In the 1980s, during what has been referred to as the cola wars, soft-drink manufacturer Pepsi ran a series of advertisements where people, caught on hidden camera, in a blind taste test, chose Pepsi over rival Coca-Cola.

a. 28-hour day
b. 33 Strategies of War
c. 1990 Clean Air Act
d. Comparative advertising

Chapter 11. The Buyer's Order and Vendor Relations 37

12. _____, known in the United States as antitrust law, has three main elements:

- prohibiting agreements or practices that restrict free trading and competition between business entities. This includes in particular the repression of cartels.
- banning abusive behavior by a firm dominating a market, or anti-competitive practices that tend to lead to such a dominant position. Practices controlled in this way may include predatory pricing, tying, price gouging, refusal to deal, and many others.
- supervising the mergers and acquisitions of large corporations, including some joint ventures. Transactions that are considered to threaten the competitive process can be prohibited altogether, or approved subject to 'remedies' such as an obligation to divest part of the merged business or to offer licenses or access to facilities to enable other businesses to continue competing.

The substance and practice of _____ varies from jurisdiction to jurisdiction. Protecting the interests of consumers (consumer welfare) and ensuring that entrepreneurs have an opportunity to compete in the market economy are often treated as important objectives. _____ is closely connected with law on deregulation of access to markets, state aids and subsidies, the privatization of state owned assets and the establishment of independent sector regulators. In recent decades, _____ has been viewed as a way to provide better public services.

   a. Rulemaking
   b. Federal Employers Liability Act
   c. Right to Financial Privacy Act
   d. Competition law

13. _____ is a retail channel for the distribution of goods and services. At a basic level it may be defined as marketing and selling products, direct to consumers away from a fixed retail location. Sales are typically made through party plan, one to one demonstrations, and other personal contact arrangements.
   a. 33 Strategies of War
   b. 1990 Clean Air Act
   c. 28-hour day
   d. Direct selling

14. The _____ requires the Federal government to investigate and pursue trusts, companies and organizations suspected of violating the Act. It was the first United States Federal statute to limit cartels and monopolies, and today still forms the basis for most antitrust litigation by the federal government.
   a. 1990 Clean Air Act
   b. 28-hour day
   c. 33 Strategies of War
   d. Sherman Antitrust Act

15. An _____ is an organization founded and funded by businesses that operate in a specific industry. An industry trade association participates in public relations activities such as advertising, education, political donations, lobbying and publishing, but its main focus is collaboration between companies, or standardization. Associations may offer other services, such as producing conferences, networking or charitable events or offering classes or educational materials.

   a. A4e
   b. A Stake in the Outcome
   c. Industry trade group
   d. AAAI

Chapter 12. Pricing and Selling

1. _____ is one of the four Ps of the marketing mix. The other three aspects are product, promotion, and place. It is also a key variable in microeconomic price allocation theory.
   a. Penetration pricing
   b. Pricing
   c. Transfer pricing
   d. Price floor

2. _____ is one of the managerial functions like planning, organizing, staffing and directing. It is an important function because it helps to check the errors and to take the corrective action so that deviation from standards are minimized and stated goals of the organization are achieved in desired manner. According to modern concepts, _____ is a foreseeing action whereas earlier concept of _____ was used only when errors were detected. _____ in management means setting standards, measuring actual performance and taking corrective action.
   a. Schedule of reinforcement
   b. Turnover
   c. Decision tree pruning
   d. Control

3. _____ is the difference between the cost of a good or service and its selling price. A _____ is added on to the total cost incurred by the producer of a good or service in order to create a profit. The total cost reflects the total amount of both fixed and variable expenses to produce and distribute a product.
   a. Markup
   b. Price points
   c. Premium pricing
   d. Topics

4. _____, net margin, net _____ or net profit ratio all refer to a measure of profitability. It is calculated by finding the net profit as a percentage of the revenue.

$$\text{Net profit margin} = \frac{\text{Net profit (after taxes)}}{\text{Revenue}} \times 100\%$$

The _____ is mostly used for internal comparison.

   a. Profit maximization
   b. Net profit margin
   c. Profit margin
   d. 1990 Clean Air Act

Chapter 12. Pricing and Selling

5. _____ is a lightweight markup language, originally created by John Gruber and Aaron Swartz to help maximum readability and 'publishability' of both its input and output forms. The language takes many cues from existing conventions for marking up plain text in email. _____ converts its marked-up text input to valid, well-formed XHTML and replaces left-pointing angle brackets ('<') and ampersands with their corresponding character entity references.
   a. 28-hour day
   b. 1990 Clean Air Act
   c. 33 Strategies of War
   d. Markdown

6. _____, Gross profit margin or Gross Profit Rate can be defined as the amount of contribution to the business enterprise, after paying for direct-fixed and direct-variable unit costs, required to cover overheads (fixed commitments) and provide a buffer for unknown items. It expresses the relationship between gross profit and sales revenue.

It can be expressed in absolute terms:

Gross Profit = Revenue − Cost of Sales

or as the ratio of gross profit to sales revenue, usually in the form of a percentage:

_____ Percentage = (Revenue-Cost of Sales)/Revenue

Cost of Sales includes variable costs and fixed costs directly linked to the product, such as material and labor.

   a. 1990 Clean Air Act
   b. Gross margin
   c. Profit maximization
   d. Profit margin

7. In accounting, _____ or sales profit is the difference between revenue and the cost of making a product or providing a service, before deducting overhead, payroll, taxation, and interest payments. Note that this is different from operating profit (earnings before interest and taxes.)

Net sales are calculated:

   Net sales = Sales - Sales returns and allowances.

Chapter 12. Pricing and Selling

a. Cash flow
b. Gross profit margin
c. Gross profit
d. Capital budgeting

8. In business and finance accounting, _____ is equal to the gross profit minus overheads minus interest payable plus/minus one off items for a given time period (usually: accounting period.)

A common synonym for '_____' when discussing financial statements (which include a balance sheet and an income statement) is the bottom line. This term results from the traditional appearance of an income statement which shows all allocated revenues and expenses over a specified time period with the resulting summation on the bottom line of the report.

a. Matching principle
b. Net profit
c. Treasury stock
d. Generally accepted accounting principles

9. _____ is a measure of a company's earning power from ongoing operations, equal to earnings before the deduction of interest payments and income taxes.

To accountants, economic profit, or EP, is a single-period metric to determine the value created by a company in one period - usually a year. It is the net profit after tax less the equity charge, a risk-weighted cost of capital.

a. A Stake in the Outcome
b. Operating profit
c. AAAI
d. A4e

10. A _____ is a government- or group-imposed limit on how low a price can be charged for a product. In order for a _____ to be effective, it must be greater than the equilibrium price. An ineffective _____, below equilibrium price.

A _____ can be set below the free-market equilibrium price.

a. Transfer pricing
b. Pricing objectives
c. Price floor
d. Penetration pricing

11. A _____ is typically described as a deliberate plan of action to guide decisions and achieve rational outcome(s.) However, the term may also be used to denote what is actually done, even though it is unplanned.

The term may apply to government, private sector organizations and groups, and individuals.

a. 33 Strategies of War
b. 1990 Clean Air Act
c. Policy
d. 28-hour day

12. In economics, business, retail, and accounting, a _____ is the value of money that has been used up to produce something, and hence is not available for use anymore. In economics, a _____ is an alternative that is given up as a result of a decision. In business, the _____ may be one of acquisition, in which case the amount of money expended to acquire it is counted as _____.

a. Cost
b. Cost overrun
c. Cost allocation
d. Fixed costs

13. _____ is an advertisement in which a particular product specifically mentions a competitor by name for the express purpose of showing why the competitor is inferior to the product naming it.

This should not be confused with parody advertisements, where a fictional product is being advertised for the purpose of poking fun at the particular advertisement, nor should it be confused with the use of a coined brand name for the purpose of comparing the product without actually naming an actual competitor. ('Wikipedia tastes better and is less filling than the Encyclopedia Galactica.')

In the 1980s, during what has been referred to as the cola wars, soft-drink manufacturer Pepsi ran a series of advertisements where people, caught on hidden camera, in a blind taste test, chose Pepsi over rival Coca-Cola.

a. 33 Strategies of War
b. Comparative advertising
c. 1990 Clean Air Act
d. 28-hour day

14. A _____ is a list of the general tasks and responsibilities of a position. Typically, it also includes to whom the position reports, specifications such as the qualifications needed by the person in the job, salary range for the position, etc. A _____ is usually developed by conducting a job analysis, which includes examining the tasks and sequences of tasks necessary to perform the job.
    a. Recruitment Process Insourcing
    b. Job description
    c. Recruitment
    d. Recruitment advertising

Chapter 1
1. b 2. d 3. d 4. c 5. d 6. d 7. d 8. b 9. c 10. d
11. d 12. a 13. b 14. a 15. d

Chapter 2
1. d 2. c 3. c 4. a 5. d 6. a 7. d 8. d

Chapter 3
1. d 2. a 3. d 4. a 5. b 6. d 7. d 8. d 9. a 10. d
11. d 12. d 13. d 14. a 15. c 16. d 17. c

Chapter 4
1. a 2. c 3. d 4. d 5. d 6. d 7. d 8. d 9. b

Chapter 5
1. d 2. d 3. d 4. a 5. c 6. d

Chapter 6
1. d 2. d 3. b 4. d 5. d 6. b 7. a 8. d 9. d 10. d
11. b 12. d 13. a

Chapter 7
1. d 2. c 3. d 4. c 5. b 6. d

Chapter 8
1. d 2. b 3. d 4. a 5. d 6. c 7. b 8. d 9. d

Chapter 9
1. a 2. a 3. a 4. d 5. a 6. d 7. d 8. c 9. c 10. c

Chapter 10
1. b 2. d 3. b 4. d 5. b 6. d 7. d 8. c 9. a 10. d
11. a 12. d 13. a 14. c

Chapter 11
1. c 2. b 3. d 4. d 5. a 6. d 7. d 8. b 9. c 10. d
11. d 12. d 13. d 14. d 15. c

Chapter 12
1. b 2. d 3. a 4. c 5. d 6. b 7. c 8. b 9. b 10. c
11. c 12. a 13. b 14. b

www.ingramcontent.com/pod-product-compliance
Lightning Source LLC
Chambersburg PA
CBHW080744250426
43671CB00038B/2867